How to Make Wonderful Porcelain Beads and Jewelry

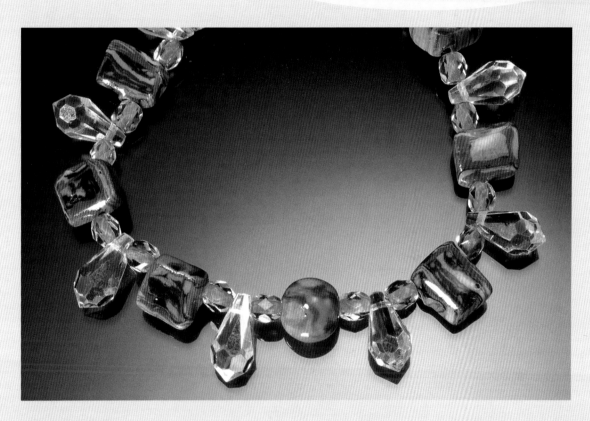

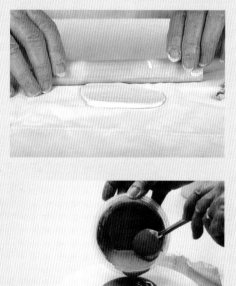

Vicki Kahn

Schiffer Publishing Ltd

4880 Lower Valley Road, Atglen, PA 19310 USA

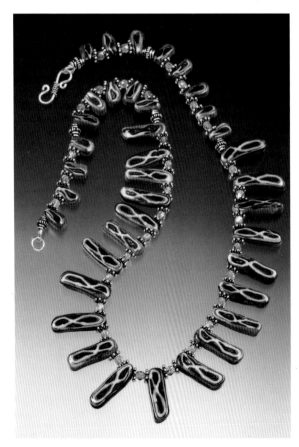

Designed by "Sue"
Type set in Seagull Hv BT/Humanist 521 BT

ISBN: 0-7643-2377-6
Printed in China

Published by Schiffer Publishing Ltd.
4880 Lower Valley Road
Atglen, PA 19310
Phone: (610) 593-1777; Fax: (610) 593-2002
E-mail: Info@schifferbooks.com

For the largest selection of fine reference books on
this and related subjects, please visit our web site at
www.schifferbooks.com
We are always looking for people to write books on
new and related subjects. If you have an idea for a
book please contact us at the above address.

This book may be purchased from the publisher.
Include $3.95 for shipping.
Please try your bookstore first.
You may write for a free catalog.

In Europe, Schiffer books are distributed by
Bushwood Books
6 Marksbury Ave.
Kew Gardens
Surrey TW9 4JF England
Phone: 44 (0) 20 8392-8585; Fax: 44 (0) 20 8392-
9876
E-mail: info@bushwoodbooks.co.uk
Free postage in the U.K., Europe; air mail at cost.

Dedication

To my family
My four children and six grandchildren have
     contributed to this book by being encour-
     aging and supportive and loving.
I am so proud of this dynasty!

Acknowledgments

I could not have brought this document to life without the help of the following persons: Emily Jones, Marty Starr, Liz Hill, Bea Solomon, Barb Hayes, Ann Keech, Sandy Eisdorfer, Sandy Mills, Sandy and Joe McMahan, Merv and Dinah Kerzner, Diane Zweben, Nancy Wambach, Jeff Snyder, Al and Rainey Kanter, Kathleen Hughes, Connie McAuliffe, Sig Melton, Andy Kahn, Jeff Kahn, Claudia Fonda, Amy Kahn, and the countless others who entered my life at various pinpoints, contributed, and then left.

Contents

Preface –
Including a Short Biography of the Author

Included in this book of detailed instructions for the making of bead jewelry with that most sensuous of materials, porcelain, are short accounts of a variety of travels during twenty-five years. I want to share with my readers some thoughts on an artist's growth in life's journey. A thread of clay tugged me to Medieval French castles and ancient, walled villages and to the people and ghosts who lived there. An encounter in a Dutch museum and a view of primitive pottery village Mata Ortiz enriched my understanding of other cultures. I changed and grew and my choice became a happy decision.

My Uncle Joe across the street was a book collector. As a child I chose often to go to his apartment where I could look through art books with colorful pictures. I don't think I understood them but I remember being enchanted with the colors. My mother taught me what she knew about needlework and I was in love with colored threads and yarns. My further introduction to art was as designer of paper doll clothes. I entered the art world as a Retailing Major and enrolled in several art classes. Two-dimensional painting was unsatisfying. I kept painting with a heavy brush, finally layering the paint on from tube to canvas. When I was nineteen a friend suggested that we go to a beginner's pottery class down in Greenwich Village in New York City. When I touched clay for the first time a light bulb went on in my head and goose bumps surged down my neck. That was an epiphany, and when I realized that I was in the wrong medium, I put away my paints and brushes. I spent as much time as I could making pots. It was the beginning of fifty years of exploration of the clay experience. Along this road I met my first mentor, Miss Halperin, my art teacher. She insisted that I learn the basics, yet encouraged experimentation, a key to her philosophy. Her Mantra, "What if?," became my own.

Another friend suggested that I apply to summer camps as a ceramics counselor. My second mentor was Mrs. Geedy Hirsch, who wished to observe me teaching a class. I had never taught anything to anybody but Mrs. Hirsch judged me on my enthusiasm and skills in teaching children as more unique than my general knowledge of clay. To my surprise she hired me to design a new ceramics studio, and teach classes in her girl's summer camp. Later I would learn that I was being nudged toward teaching Art by a Professor of Education at Columbia University. Camp Romaca was a fabulous growth experience, and I spent two summers working and learning. I realized that my passion for clay needed to be financially supported. The immutable fact was that to be happy I needed clay under my nails. I enrolled in New York University's Art Education program. I would be able to have my clay and get paid for teaching as well.

Two years later I was engaged to be married, with a year left to get my BS in Art Education with a Minor in Crafts. That summer I was awarded a summer scholarship to Alfred University's School of Ceramics. It was another enriching experience. We moved to Stamford, Connecticut, a year before I graduated and I commuted to NYC to do my practice teaching and complete my course work. Later I taught Art in the Stamford School District and also adult pottery classes.

By then I had permanent clay under my nails. I took ten years off to raise my four children but never stopped working in clay. Being an art teacher gave me time off during the summer and as my children became more self-sufficient I discovered interesting ways to develop my passion. Theme vacations and workshops both here and abroad enriched my experience.

Years later, a big change came into my life when I was granted a year long travel sabbatical by my employer, a county agency providing special services to all special needs students. My husband and I bought a motor home. It was very comfortable but had no room for the pottery I was then making. The solution was to miniaturize. Making porcelain bead jewelry rose out of necessity and was the right decision at the right time.

Holland

One year my husband and I spent a month in the Netherlands. He was developing a new typewriter in Holland and I was able to take the time to go with him. I traveled by myself during the day while he was working and in the evening told him all about my adventures. One day I explored the Utrecht Museum. The area was not lit and there were boxes everywhere, waiting for a new show to be set up. Suddenly a young bearded curator came up and said I had to come back next week when the show was open. I said I wouldn't be there next week, I was a potter from America, and very interested in pottery. Pottery is one of those universal words and the curator invited me to come look at the pottery in his workshop. Construction of a new Convention Center had unearthed Roman pots. These were the rejects of a kiln firing and the curator wanted to know if I could identify them and what their function might be. Yes, I would be delighted to do that and spent a wonderful forty-five minutes in that workroom.

Le Moulin

Browsing in a *Ceramics Monthly* my eye caught an ad describing a pottery workshop in Burgundy, France. I researched *Fodor*, arranged for air tickets and a Parisian hotel, and wrote to Le Moulin to tell them I was coming.

The light is what you notice first. The luminous skylight that attracted the Impressionists to Burgundy 100 years ago was the same light that enthralled me the summer of 1983. Almost lost in the hills less than 100 miles from Paris lies the tiny village of Pouilly-sur-Serein. Phillip Gearheart and his wife, Hester, purchased and remodeled an abandoned old grain mill into a painting and pottery studio, with dormitories under the eaves for sixteen students. Le Moulin attracted a continental student body and offered a charming blend of creative handwork, fine dining, an international atmosphere, and a very unique lifestyle. Poilly, with its 250 permanent residents, is timeless. Its buildings are old, its farms prosperous, and its traditions formed by continuity rather than change. All shops and services shut down between 11:45 and 2:15. Everyone comes home for a traditional French dinner, served one course at a time with copious quantities of Burgundian *van ordinaire*. The villagers make the wine for their own use, not for export. The cheeses too, served at every meal, are locally made.

Our day began with a continental breakfast followed by an intense period of concentrated creative work. Phil Gearheart spent an hour with each student, discussing the student's goals for the two weeks course. My decision was to make porcelain hand built castles because they were a challenge and intrigued me. The results delighted me and I carried home the three best.

On Sunday, our only free day, painters and potters alike visited the nearby ancient sites of Burgundy. We joined the French Mass at the 800-year-old cathedral at Vezelay and afterwards looked down from the ramparts onto the fields from which Eleanor of Aquitaine and her husband, Louis VII, departed for Jerusalem during the Second Crusade. Auxerre is an ancient city unknown to most of us. Here Thomas a Becket came to be educated and Attila the Hun was stopped from invading Paris. Joan of Arc prayed here at the Cathedral of St. Etienne.

My images of Le Moulin and Poilly do not fade; the cows crossing the Serein every morning; the parties in the Gearheart's rose garden, and Bastille Day in Poilly; the little epicerie that stocked one of everything that a villager might want or need; and the final unstacking of the big gas kiln on our last night and the serious evaluations. Like Camelot it only rained at night and my images are golden with that warm Burgundian sun. The celadon porcelain castles are a treasure that serve as a reminder of a very stimulating and rewarding summer.

Mata Ortiz

We were in the third world for New Year's weekend 2001 and looking forward to an adventurous experience. Juan Quezada is the guiding light behind some of the finest pottery being made today. Now middle aged, he has become world renowned in pottery circles. This uneducated man discovered some ancient Casas Grandes shards while in the mountains around his village. He was fascinated by the patterns still visible on this one thousand year old pottery. His curiosity and determination prevailed through many years of trial and error, since there was no tradition of pottery making in Mata Ortiz. He discovered how to make wonderful, expressive pots following traditional designs. He discovered the right combination of red clay and yellow clay. When the clay cracked during firing, he found he had to add other materials like volcanic ash to temper the clay. After many efforts, he began to produce very fine work, created only by the most traditional methods. He buys nothing. Tools and materials come from the earth. They work as well as, or better than, the most sophisticated ones found in pottery catalogs. The pots are burnished with stones and then fine, intricate patterns are drawn onto the pot.

He uses no compasses or calipers, no paper patterns. His ideas are in his head and are transmitted from head to hand by his heart. He is sincere, dedicated, and as driven as any other passionate potter. He uses a brush made from stiff human hair wrapped around a stick. He has a steady hand and draws his designs with precision. When done, he will use another brush and some clay slip in another color and make sweeping, swirling lines which segment the pot into quadrants. When he is satisfied with the decoration he fires the pot. Three spokes are driven into the ground. The pot is placed on them to keep it off the ground. A large garden urn is placed over it and dried cow dung is packed all arond the pot. It is wrapped in baling wire and kerosene is poured over the base and set afire. After forty-five minutes the fire burns itself out and the pot cools. A few hours later it is unveiled and it is perfect! A marvel if it had come out of a kiln but this marvel is made by the most primitive methods and it takes your breath away. Juan Quezada has a great reputation as a fine, world-class potter, but this man, perhaps because of his humble origins, is unpretentious, warm, and friendly.

He has taught all of his siblings – he has ten – and many of them are achieving reputations. Now his children have taken up the standard and they, too, will develop fine pots. The dusty village still doesn't have paved streets but now it has electricity and running water. Some of the houses sport dish antennas and TV's. Many kitchens have microwaves. It is claimed that there are now more pick up trucks than burros. We gringos with fat wallets have been improving the economy of Mata Ortiz for only five or ten years. It's exciting to be part of the changes. In addition to Juan, our weekend included visits to many other potters and observing demonstrations. The houses are small by Western standards and a typical house had pottery everywhere, on beds, sofas, and tables. The pottery studio is usually a table set up in a bedroom.

Olivia Rodriguez demonstrated constructing a pot. She took a lump of clay and rolled it out with a PVC plastic roller. She called this the tortilla. Someone in our group commented that she was making empenadas. She said she was too busy making pots to make empenadas. She placed the tortilla in a clay form and pressed and molded it until it was smooth using her hands and a broken shard. Then she rolled a thick coil she called a chorizo, a word for Mexican sausage. This coil was firmly attached and pressed upward to form the body and shoulder of the pot. When she was satisfied with the form, she added another smaller coil for the lip of the pot. The pot is then set aside until it dries. When dry, it will be burnished with a stone and painted.

Olivia's husband, Armando, showed us how the clay is refined for working. It is brought down from the mountains in big chunks and put in large buckets of water to soak. When the clay is totally soaked, it is poured over a cloth so that the clay slurry goes through the cloth while all the stones and other debris remain on top. This process is repeated several times. The clarified clay is then poured onto a plaster trough to dry. Then the clay is made into balls and wrapped in plastic sheets.

All weekend we were treated to demonstrations of painting or sculpting. At one stop, a lovely lady named Debi Bishop showed us her javelina sculptures. They were charming and already fired, but needed to be smoked and their snouts sanded. We bought some and later that evening her husband delivered them to the inn. The interesting thing about Debi was that she spoke perfect English. When I asked her about that she said she came from Phoenix, Arizona, and had been married before. She came to Mata Ortiz with three children. Then she married a Mexican and had three more children, and is very, very happy with her decision.

Gloria Hernandez was an energetic, strong personality with a constant smile and an infectious laugh. After many purchases from our crowd – one shelf of pots virtually disappeared – she invited all of us into her kitchen for tamales. That is a New Year's tradition in Mexico. There were several huge bowls of tamales. She heated about a dozen in her microwave and served them on paper plates along with cans of local Tecate beer. Another insight into the Mexican soul is the generosity of these simple people. The next day, on our way north, we stopped in Old Casas Grandes to visit Nicholas Quezada, a brother of Juan's. He had a beautiful house decorated very well in the Mexican style. He showed us a handsome pot designed to be sold for eight hundred dollars. Unfortunately, the base had developed a bubble in firing and was considered defective. But one of our group bought it for one hundred dollars. Another stop was Lydia Quezada, Juan's sister. She made stunning pots and everyone seemed to buy. On leaving Lydia's house, I was stopped by a strange man who first shook my hand and then hugged and kissed me. It was another New Year's tradition in Mexico.

Roman pot, 1ˢᵗ or 2ⁿᵈ Century BC. *Courtesy of the University of Pennsylvania Museum.*

Roman pot, 1ˢᵗ or 2ⁿᵈ Century BC. *Courtesy of the University of Pennsylvania Museum.*

Le Moulin main quarters.

Roman pot, 1ˢᵗ or 2ⁿᵈ Century BC. *Courtesy of the University of Pennsylvania Museum.*

Street in Poilly-sur-Serene.

Impressionist view from dorm.

Porcelain interpretation of Vezelay
created by Vicki Kahn.

French postcard of
Cathedral at Vezelay.

Celadon porcelain castle created by Vicki Kahn.

Pot on stand waiting for fire.

Gloria Rodriquez making a coiled pot.

Juan Quesada explaining clay additives.

The fire burning for forty-five minutes.

Juan Quesada signing book for Vicki Kahn.

Preparing the clay.

Debie Bishop Bugarini.

Beads have been around since the dawn of time. Any visit to an anthropological museum will display beads used for ornamentation and trade. They have been made from diverse materials such as bones, glass, shells, gems, and rocks. Chances are they were not made from porcelain.

Today, porcelain has been discovered as the bead of choice among experienced bead makers. Bead artists like the dense molecular structure that makes it such a hard, durable material and its amazing affinity for color. Until quite recently, little was available in the literature about creating por-

celain beads. The interest in FIMO (a polyvinyl chloride) has produced some excellent books on forming FIMO beads. One I particularly like is *The New Clay* by Nan Roche. Although written for FIMO, it is a superb instruction book for porcelain beads.

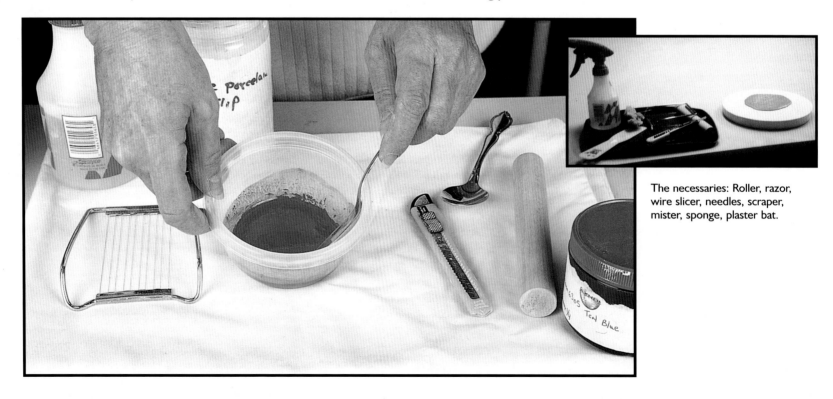

The necessaries: Roller, razor, wire slicer, needles, scraper, mister, sponge, plaster bat.

Colored porcelain slip is not generally available in the pottery catalogs so it is necessary to develop one's own techniques. Since I am not a chemist, I follow an empirical approach. Place two tablespoons of a Mason stain of your choice in a half cup of water and mix until it becomes a smooth slurry. Then add to the mixture about two cups of white porcelain slip and mix until the color is smooth and consistent. Be aware that the firing range of all stains varies. The information you want is there in the catalog. Be sure you read all the specifications and choose only the stains that will fire successfully at 2200 degrees. Reds and pinks are notorious for burning out before the specified firing range. Recently, some makers have developed newer, more stable colors, which are available in the catalogs. These will not burn out.

Slurry mixed.

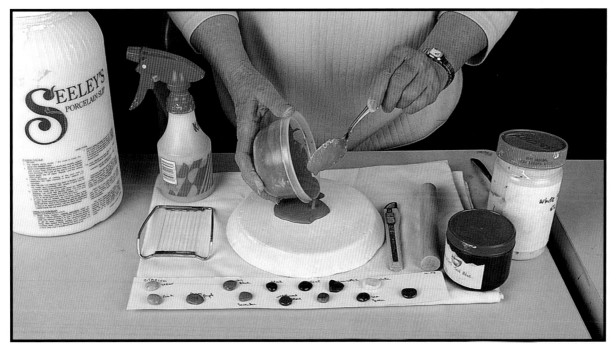

Pouring slurry onto plaster surface.

An intense color will require less slip while a bland color will require more slip. It is truly trial and error. The liquid must be dried out to form clay. One good way to do this is to put a few tablespoons of prepared slip on a dry plaster surface. When the plaster has absorbed the water it is ready for the next step. Gently peel the clay off the plaster and put it in zippered plastic bags. Label the bags with a black Sharpie pen.

Select three or four complementary colors. Select one color and roll out a sheet of clay to about 1/4" thick and 2- to 5-inches long and 2-inches wide. Spray the slab with a mist of water and put a sheet of plastic wrap over it. Spray each slab of colored slip in this fashion. Layer each slab until you have a colorful sandwich. Lay one slab on top of another, making sure each layer is misted. Roll over the entire color bar to ensure good adhesion.

Slice through the bar so that you have a solid rectangle 1" wide by 5" long. Place one section upon the other, being certain you have misted the entire surface. To assure even sections, place an egg slicer on the color bar and just mark the area. Do not use the slicer to cut the clay. With your razor, slice through the marked section so that you will get even spacing. Adjust for distortion and keep all the beads under plastic wrap until you are done.

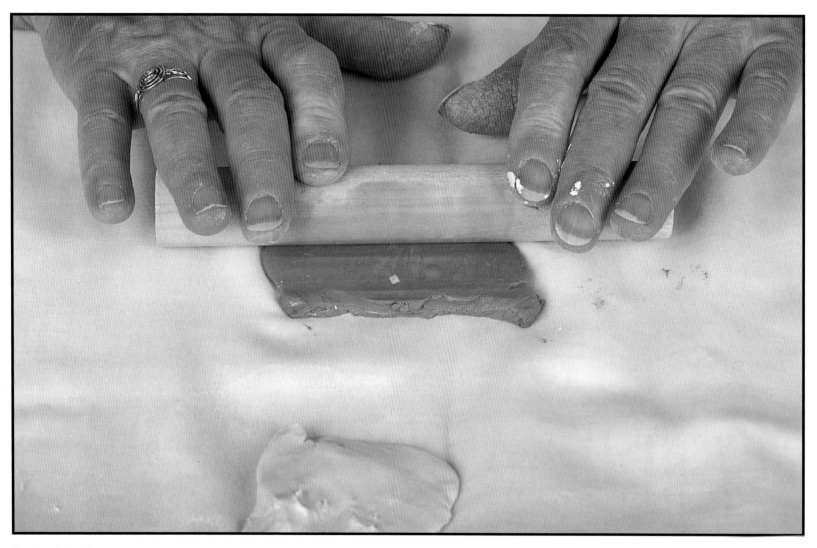

Rolling first color.

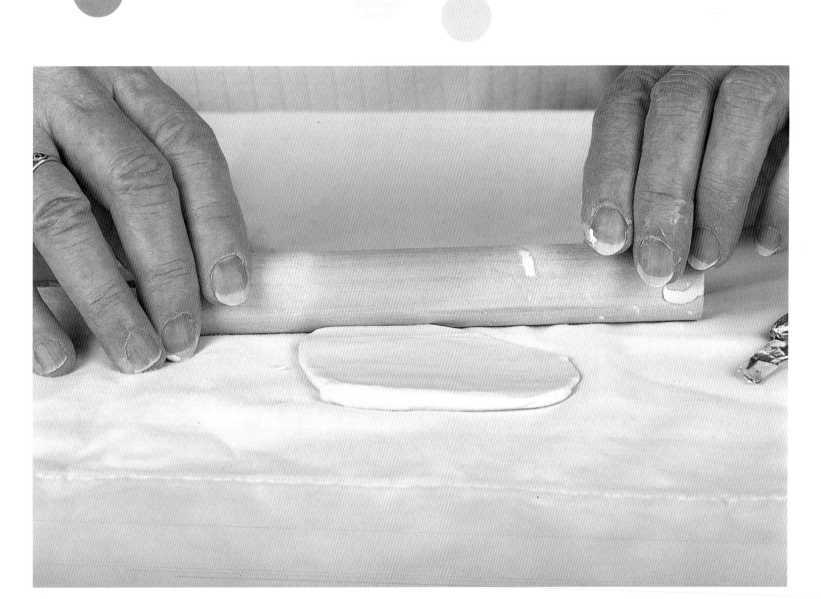

Rolling a contrasting color.

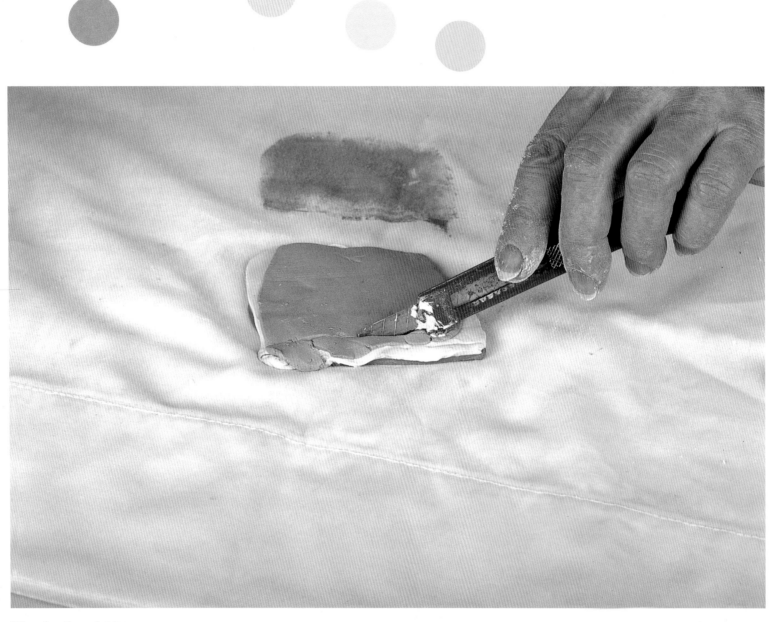

Trimming the color bar.

Color bar.

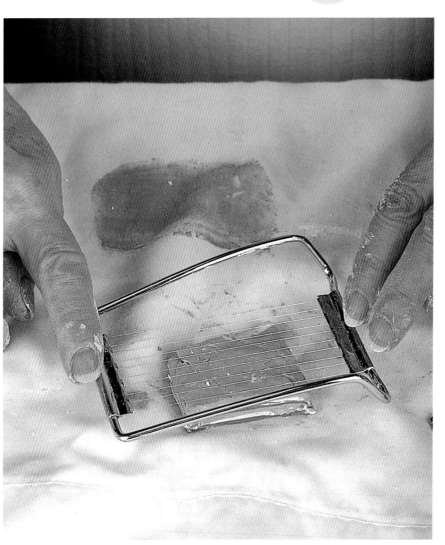

Using an egg slicer.

You must make decisions now as to what kind of bead you will make. Use a medium size darning or embroidery needle. Beads for necklaces need a horizontal hole in the top third of the soft clay bead. However, if you are making an earring bead you will need to pierce vertically through the bead with the needle. It's important to keep your beads soft at this point. Check for possible distortion of the bead shape and make sure the bead hole is open all the way through. If your beads are beginning to dry out a little, dip the needle in water first and you will find the needle works very well. If you have let them dry out too much and the beads are cracking, just spray them with water and cover the beads with plastic wrap for a while. The beads will soften and you will be able to proceed.

Dry the pierced beads thoroughly and slowly to prevent warping and cracking. Fire them in a small jewelry kiln to Cone 06 (about 1850 degrees F.) When the kiln has cooled, take out the beads and finish by sanding the rough edges or, even better, by tumbling the fired beads in a rock tumbler with water to cover them. An hour is usually about the right length of time. Check to see that the beads have no cracks and that the stringing holes are still open. Glaze with Cone 6 clear porcelain glaze on the best side of the bead. Make certain holes are not clogged with glaze and that the bottom of the bead is cleaned of all glaze. Fire to Cone 6 (about 2250 degrees F.) When cool, open the kiln and be amazed.

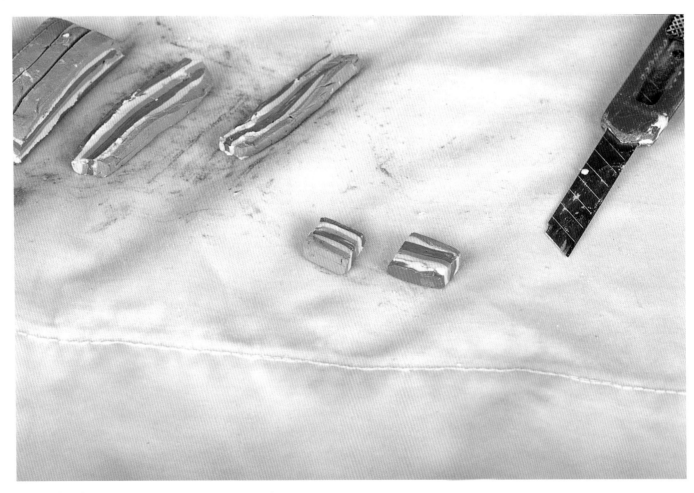

Cutting beads.

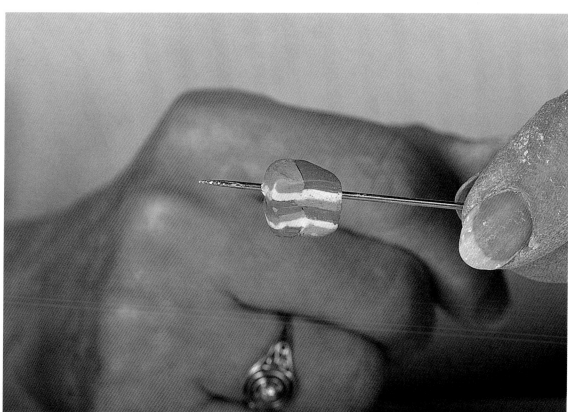

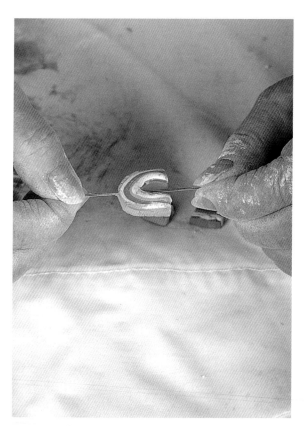

Piercing hole vertically.

Piercing hole horizontally.

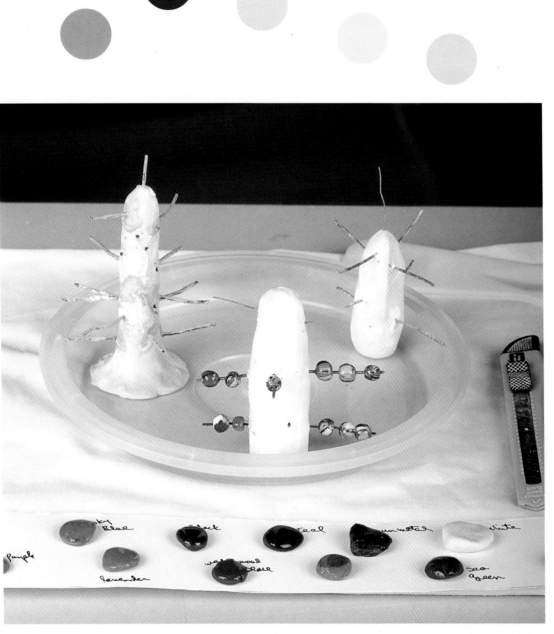

Variety of bead trees. Bead trees are one way to glaze all surfaces of your beads. I generally make my own since the commercial ones use much heavier wire than would fit into a small porcelain bead. Make stoneware cones as seen in the photo. Scoop out the center to allow for better drying.

Then cut some high temp wire, some of each gauge, 17 and 24 are generally available in the ceramic catalogs. Two gauges give you options if your bead hole is small or large.

Cut several strips of each gauge and force them into the cone. The stoneware clay will shrink some and that will hold the wire firmly in place. Let it dry thoroughly and then fire to Cone 5.

Be certain to brush a thick amount of kiln wash onto the wires before loading the bead tree. This should prevent any glaze from getting on the wires. When you brush your glaze on the bead, be careful not to get any on the wire or in the hole. There is nothing more frustrating than having a lovely bead glazed just right and frozen solid on the bead tree!

The next step is the making of the earring and necklace. This process will require a whole new set of decisions, with choices of materials and design components. Because handmade porcelain beads tend to be rough inside, I use only Softflex or Beadalon for stringing. These are nylon-coated wires that resist cutting and fraying. Lay out your best beads, using spacer beads in complementary colors, sizes, and textures. Cut your wire to size, allowing a 2" tail on each side. Fit a crimp bead on the end, followed by a clasp. When you have done that, add a drop of Hypo-cement to each crimp bead and crimp with pliers. Wear with pride!

See Chapter 4 for more complete instructions on stringing beads.

Creating earrings.

Stringing a necklace.

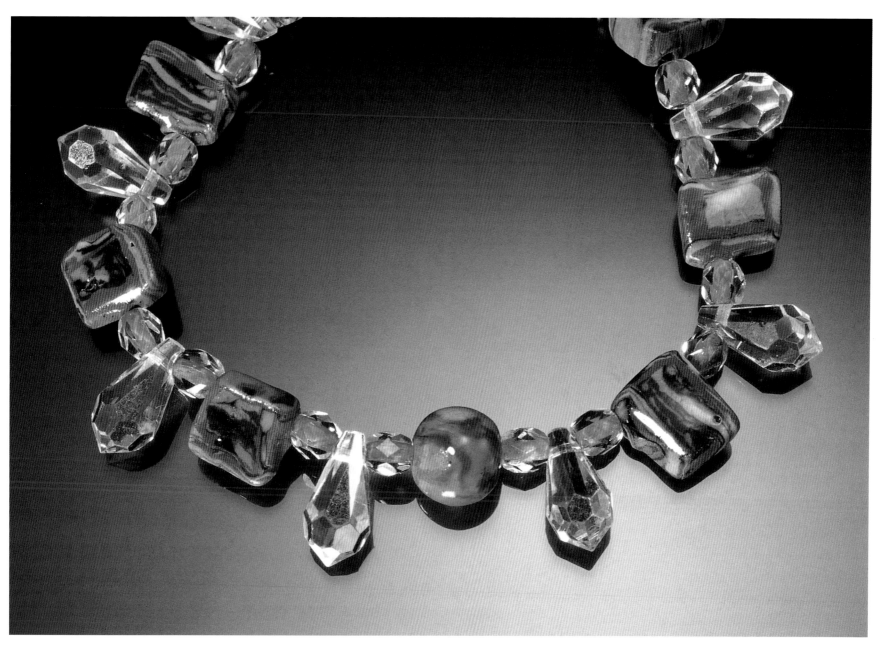

Finished necklace illustrating layered beads. *Photo courtesy of Ralph Gabriner.*

Basic Millefiori Beads

When you have achieved some competence in making the basic layered bead, you are ready to make the basic millefiori bead. Millefiori means "thousand flowers" in Italian and was developed at the beginning of the cane working technique for glass paperweights in Murano, Italy during the Middle Ages. You can now achieve your own fabulous color combinations and create your own designs. When you have mastered this technique you will have the knowledge to make any bead in any shape, size, and color combination.

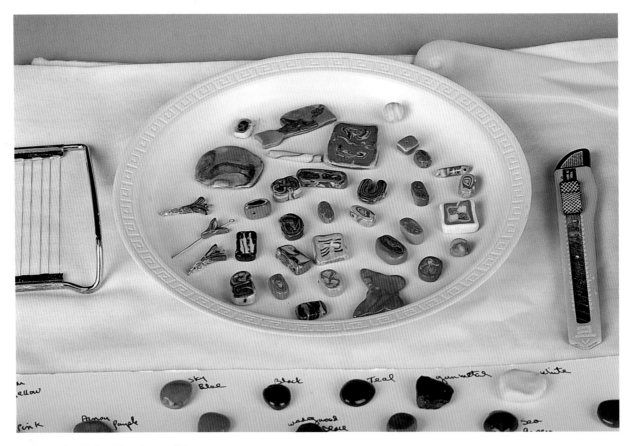

Variety of millefiori beads possible.

Select three different colored porcelain slips. Roll a thin worm shape to start, approximately 3" to 5" long. Keep it covered. Roll out a second color, it should be fairly thin. Trim the upper edge and two side edges. Mist the slab and place the thin worm at the upper edge. Carefully roll the new slab around the worm, making sure that all surfaces touch and that there are no air pockets. Cut the edge, making sure that there is no overlap. Repeat with the third color. You can repeat this process until you have a diameter of about 3/4" to 1".

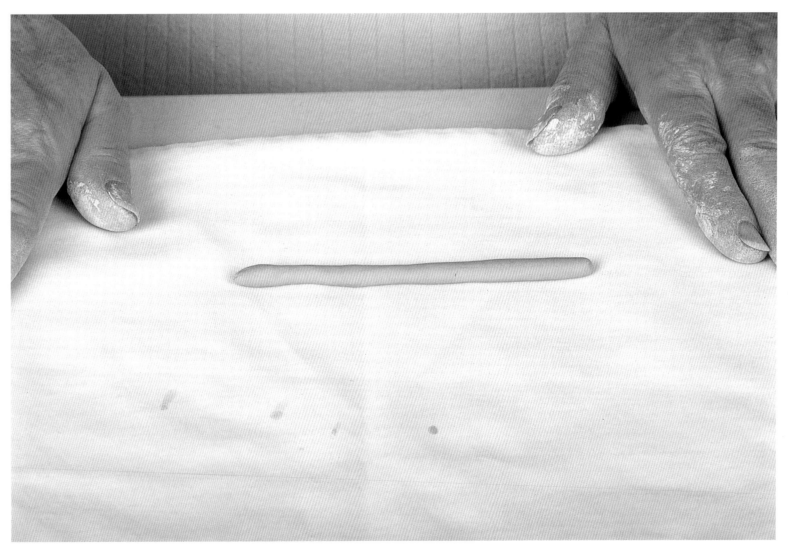

Rolling a thin worm.

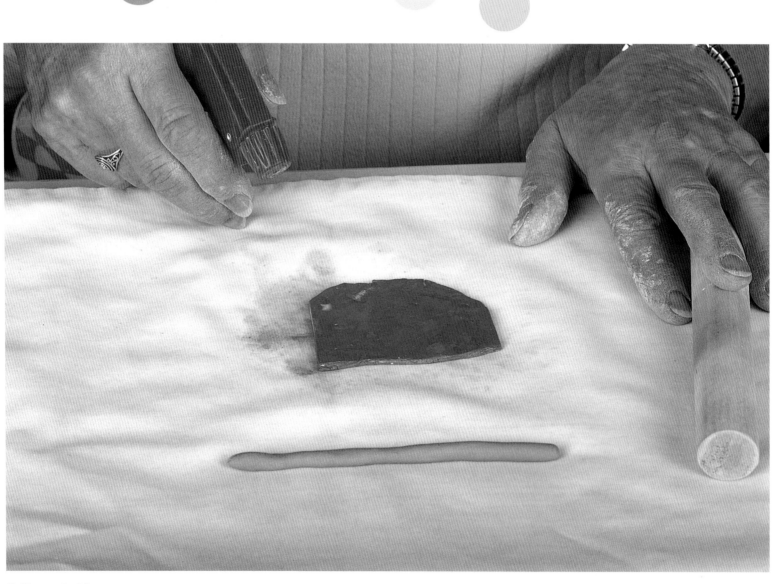

Rolling and adding worm.

Preparing for frame.

Assembling frame.

You can now create a frame around your bead using either one of the contrasting slips or using all of the scraps you have been saving and keeping moist. Roll these scraps out making sure there are no cracks in the slab and that all is moist and ready to use. There are many variations on this theme. As you become more proficient, you will find yourself inventing new forms.

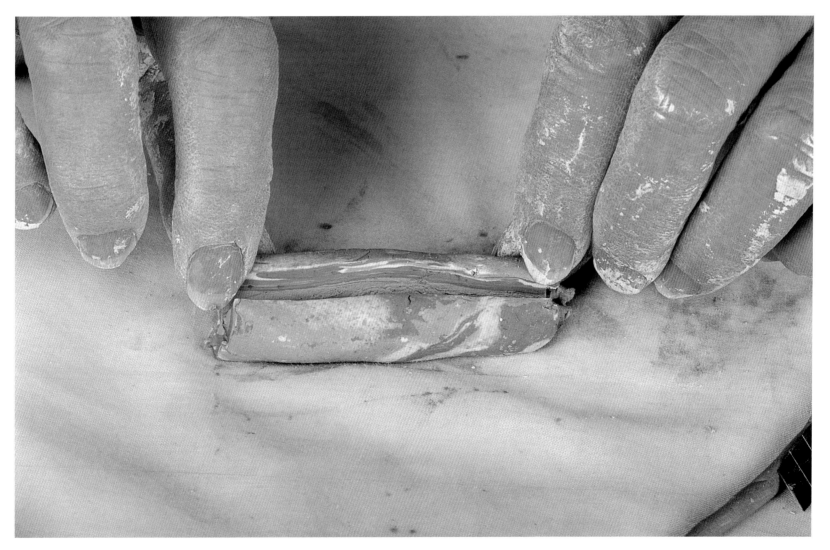

Rolling frame around core bead.

Final color roll ready for slicing.

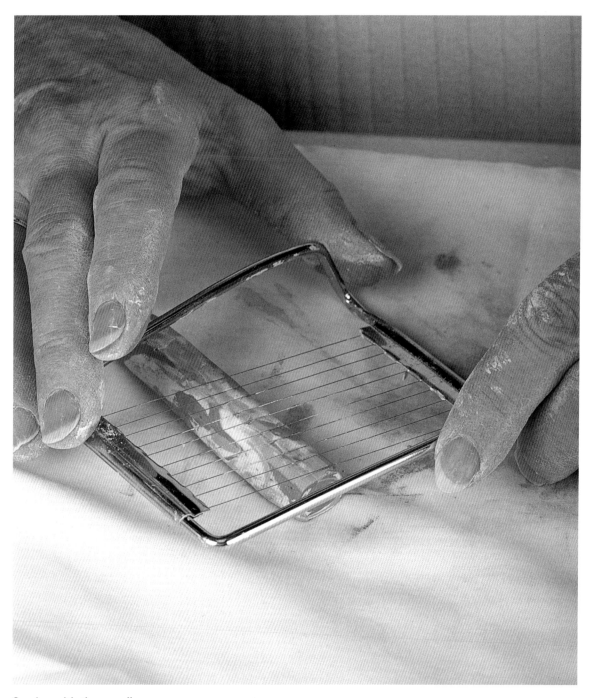

To make your basic millefiori bead, score your color roll with the egg slicer to assure uniform sizes, then cut straight down with a sharp razor tool. Do not try to cut the clay with the egg slicer; it's not sharp enough. Cut no more than three slices at a time, and keep them under plastic. For necklace beads, pull an embroidery needle through the upper third of the bead, and then reverse the process so that the eye of the needle goes through both ends. Be sure to adjust for distortion. For earring beads, make a hole from top to bottom, drawing the needle vertically through the bead and back again. Keep your finished beads under plastic. (As you may have noticed, I can't emphasize this enough. I live in Tucson, Arizona, for part of the year, and the lack of humidity in the workplace can be a problem.) Adjust for any distortion in the bead, check to see if the hole goes through, and put aside to dry. If you are having trouble pulling your needle through the bead there are two things you can do: dip your needle in water before inserting it into the bead or, if that doesn't work, mist the bead and cover with plastic. The bead was allowed to dry too much. You'll find that water is both an enemy and a friend. I assure you that you will get the hang of it and make wonderful beads.

Scoring with the egg slicer.

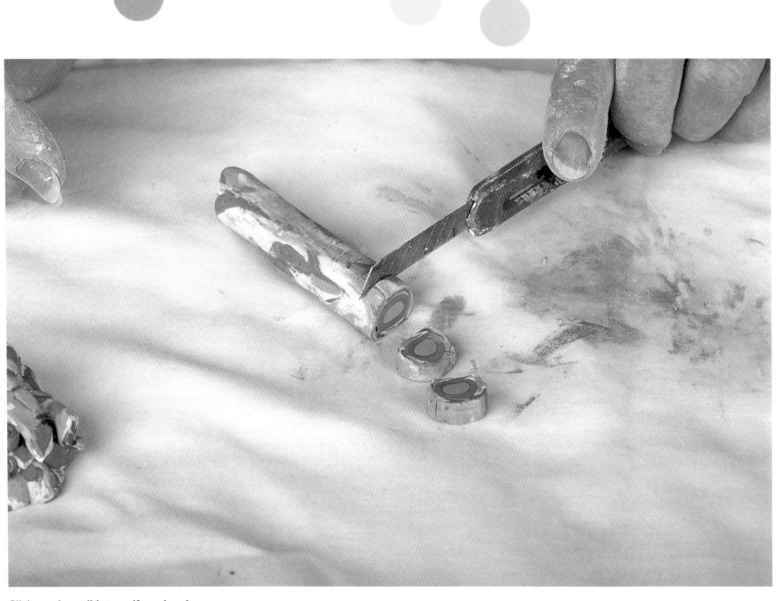

Slicing color roll into uniform beads.

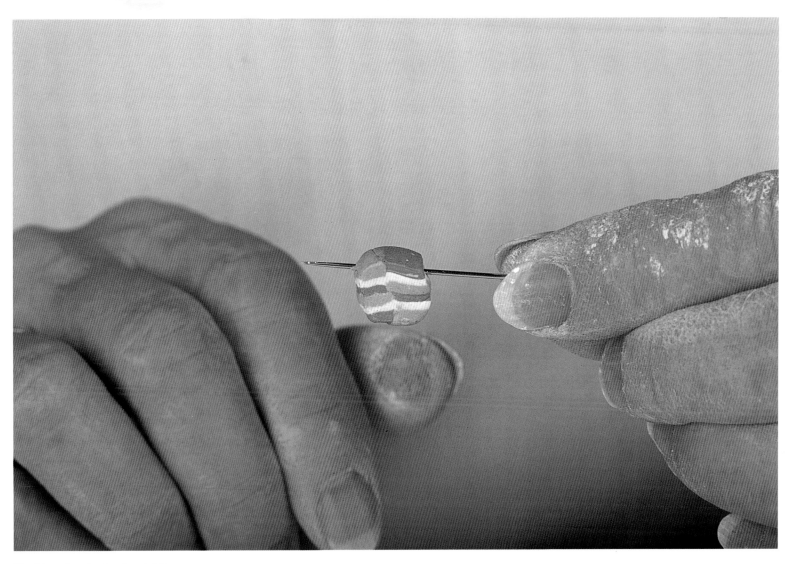

Necklace bead – horizontal line.

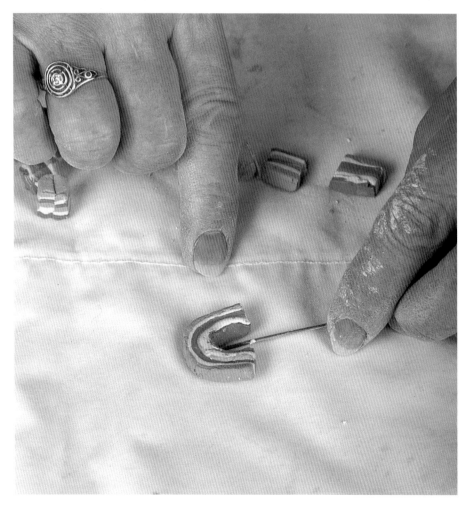

**Earring bead –
vertical line.**

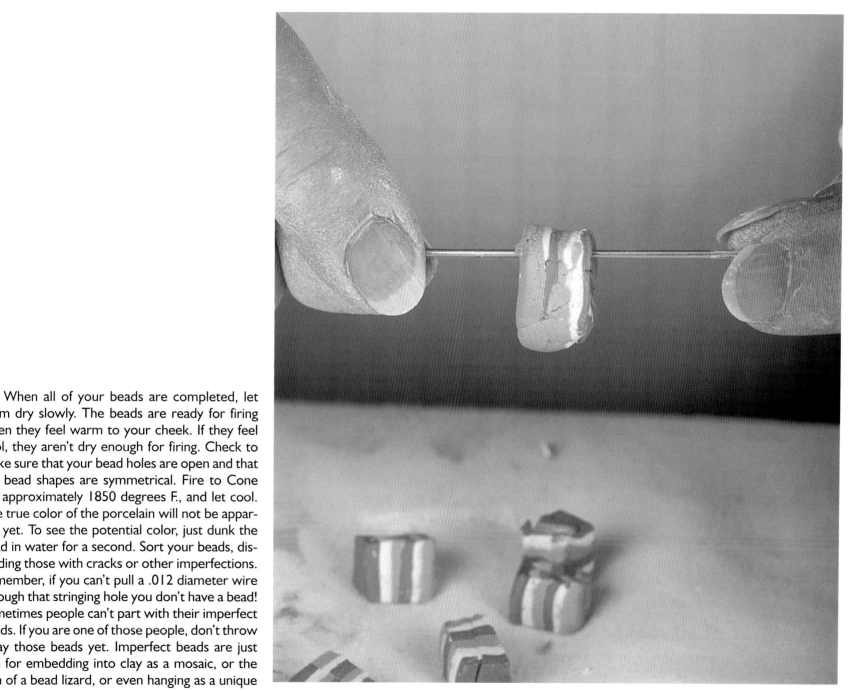

Testing bead on a stringing wire.

When all of your beads are completed, let them dry slowly. The beads are ready for firing when they feel warm to your cheek. If they feel cool, they aren't dry enough for firing. Check to make sure that your bead holes are open and that the bead shapes are symmetrical. Fire to Cone 06, approximately 1850 degrees F., and let cool. The true color of the porcelain will not be apparent yet. To see the potential color, just dunk the bead in water for a second. Sort your beads, discarding those with cracks or other imperfections. Remember, if you can't pull a .012 diameter wire through that stringing hole you don't have a bead! Sometimes people can't part with their imperfect beads. If you are one of those people, don't throw away those beads yet. Imperfect beads are just fine for embedding into clay as a mosaic, or the skin of a bead lizard, or even hanging as a unique ornament.

Finish with fine sandpaper. If you are lucky enough to have access to a rock tumbler, use it! It will save energy, time, and your fingernails. Put your beads in the tumbler with just enough water to cover the beads. No grit is necessary. Tumble for an hour and check for smoothness. Repeat if necessary until you get the smoothest result you can obtain. Rinse and dry under paper towels.

Rock tumbler.

Lay out your beads on a paper towel, best side up. Brush two coats of high-fire clear glaze on the surfaces, being careful not to clog the holes. Let dry. Make certain that the glaze doesn't drip to the underside of the beads. If it does, then wipe with a damp sponge. Fire the glazed beads to Cone 6, approximately 2200 degrees F. The firing process will take about six hours. Let cool and then open the kiln and smile! You have created an extraordinary bead.

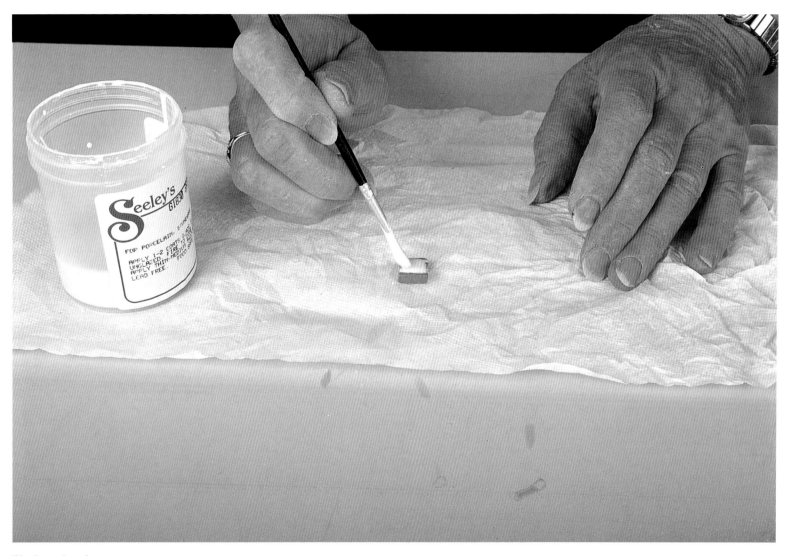

Glazing a bead.

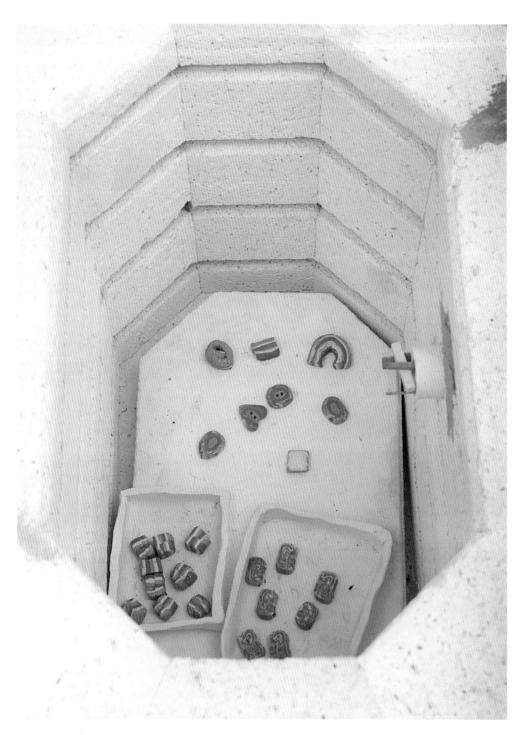

Loading the kiln.

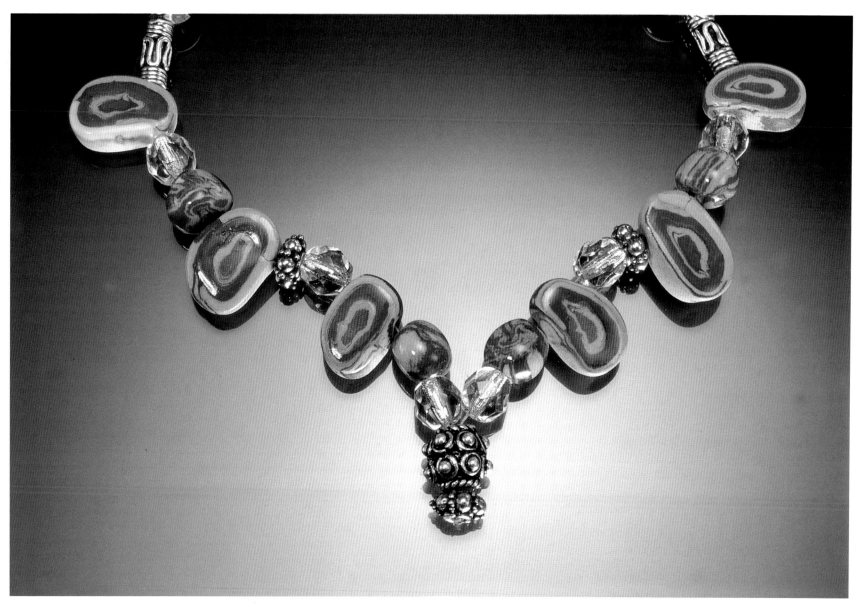

Detail of 'Rillito' necklace with millefiori beads.
Photo courtesy of Ralph Gabriner.

'Harmony' necklace of millefiori beads.
Courtesy of Steve Meltzer Photography.

Handcrafted Buttons for Your Wearable Art

Many people knit, weave or sew beautiful, finely crafted clothing. An ordinary button is not appropriate for such an elegant garment. An artistic handcrafted button will enhance any art-to-wear apparel. My material of choice is porcelain because it is durable, colorful, and sensuous. No other material is comparable. Buttons made of porcelain are machine washable (turn inside out) and dryable. The color is built in and so will not peel or chip. A porcelain button is just another kind of bead. There are many variations possible to tailor a bead or button to your special garment.

To achieve an excellent button, a very basic knowledge of the clay process is helpful. Layering is a simple technique for bead and button making. Roll out thin slabs of two different colors of porcelain clay about 2" by 4". Spray water from the mister to keep the clay moist. To layer, put one slab on top of the other. Cut in half lengthwise, mist again and roll out with a roller until the colors are blended. You should have a somewhat marbleized slab visible. You may need to experiment at this step. One suggestion is to mist the slab again and then fold it in half and roll. Your slab should be about 1/4" thick. You can vary the thickness of each color and achieve some interesting visual images.

Variety of buttons.

Another way to enhance this button is to add a border around the basic form. A word about scraps is important at this point. Never discard them because they have many functions. In addition to borders, they are useful in making spectacular beads and buttons. A little experimentation will expand your knowledge of scrap porcelain. Take some of your scraps of clay, combine and roll out into a slab the length of your color bar. Trim one edge of the slab, mist it slightly, and place the color bar at the edge. Roll the bar around the slab slowly, making sure all surfaces adhere. Do not overlap. Blend the seam edges; trim the end to see how superb your button will look.

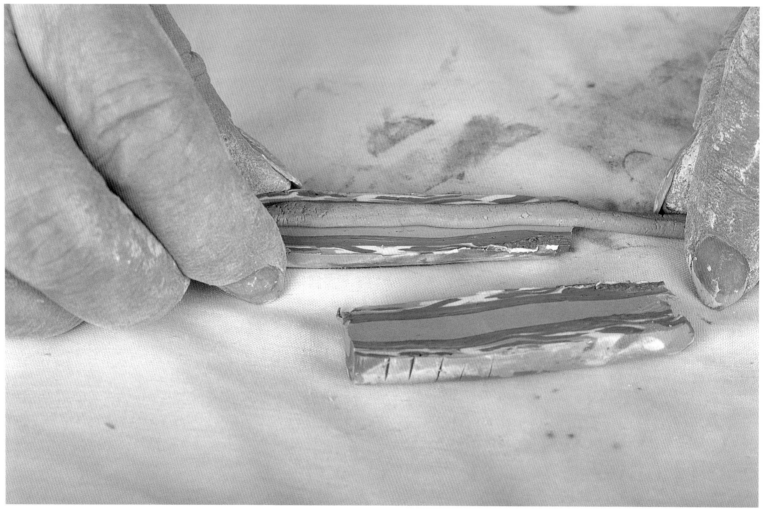

Making a border.

Place the egg slicer on the color bar to score it. Do not attempt to cut it with the slicer. Use a sharp razor and cut straight down through the color bar. Add two holes for attaching to the garment, using a toothpick or a thick darning needle. Check the other side to make sure the holes go through. Adjust for distortion, let dry and fire to Cone 06 (1850 degrees F.). When you make those sewing holes be aware that porcelain clay will shrink twenty percent!

A button constructed in the millefiori technique provides color and a very interesting pattern. Select two or three contrasting porcelain slips. Navy, pink, and crème are a good choice. Make a very thin worm of navy. Roll gently with the tips of your fingers. Now roll out a slab of crème porcelain. Trim the upper edge of the slab and set one small coil of navy right up at the edge. Remember, when adhering two pieces of clay you must moisten the surfaces. Then roll the small coil onto the slab, stopping at the edge. Do not overlap.

Cutting the buttons.

Trim the sides of the color roll so you have a neat roll. Next, roll out your pink slab and repeat the process. Let the color roll set up until it is a little firm. Use the wire egg slicer to score the roll for even slices. Do not try to use the slicer to cut the roll. With the sharp razor cut straight down until the button is separated. Put it aside and cut a few more. Keep these under plastic wrap. With a small bottle cap or lipstick tube make a slight depression in the button. This will give the button some definition. With a heavy needle or toothpick, make two equidistant holes in the button, turn it over and make sure the holes go through to the other side. Adjust for distortion and put it aside to dry, then fire to Cone 06.

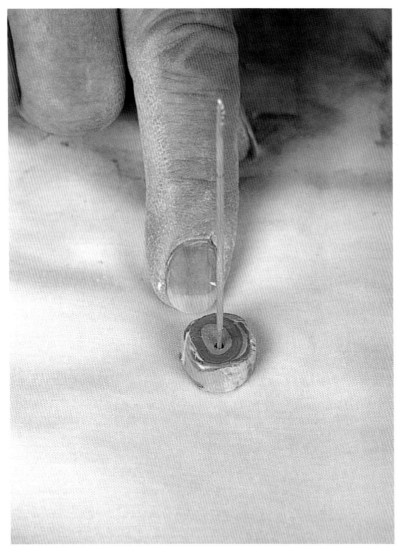

Hole placement for button.

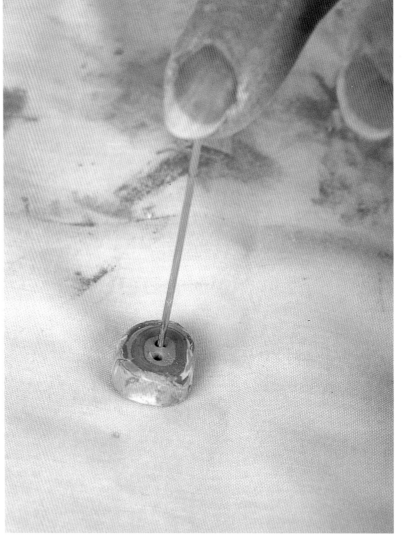

Adjusting holes.

Select shapes for buttons from hors d'oeuvres cutters. Hearts, ovals, stars, and circles are very appropriate. Use a toothpick or a heavy needle to drill two holes; then turn the button over and sand repeat on the other side. Let it dry slowly. You will know when the button is dry by holding it up to your cheek. If it is cool and damp, it is not ready to fire. When dry, place on a kiln shelf and fire for three hours at 1850 degrees F. or Cone 06.

A heart-shaped button cutout

Drilling the sewing holes.

When the kiln is cool, open and sort your buttons. A rock tumbler would be very useful at this point to smooth the rough edges. A rock tumbler will save you time, energy, and your fingernails. Tumble for about an hour with just enough water to cover the buttons. No grit is necessary.

If a tumbler is not available, sand the buttons with extra fine sandpaper. Select your best buttons and glaze with two coats of clear high fire glaze on one side only. Make sure the holes are not blocked with glaze and there is no glaze on the underside. Fire the glazed buttons to Cone 6 (2250 degrees

F.) for about six hours. When the kiln is cool, open and admire your very original buttons. Wear with pride! You have made a set of unique porcelain buttons to go with a very special handcrafted outfit.

Finished buttons.

Stringing Beads
How to Turn Your Beads Into Fabulous Jewelry

You've done the hard part and your handcrafted porcelain beads are gorgeous! Making porcelain beads from scratch is demanding and a challenge. Now the final step in this exercise is making the necklace.

Assembly is a decision-making activity. There are hundreds, even thousands of choices out there in the marketplace. How does one choose the right combination of materials to make a spectacular necklace? First, consider that there is never only one choice. There are dozens of combinations of materials that will give you a satisfying art form. Yes, your necklace is just that, an art form. Consider the combinations of color, texture, size, and materials that you might use. Assemble a few batches of materials that appeal to you. These might include Bali silver beads, crystal beads, brilliant fire polished spacers, dichroic beads or bold turquoise chips with silver hogans. If your bead has an elegant black and white stripe, you can capitalize on the monochromatic scheme and create a very sophisticated and dramatic necklace by just adding black jet crystal. Conversely, you might try pale quartz or pearls for a very different effect. Assemble three or four groups of materials that appeal to you and simply try them. String several courses of each combination onto your wire.

Don't be afraid to experiment. Remember there is no set way to assemble a necklace. It has to say something to you. When you listen to that inner voice you will know what is right for you. Then you can bring out the best components to make your necklace truly unique. Also remember that nobody is born knowing how to do this. It takes a lot of trial and error to accomplish your goal. As you grown in proficiency, your pieces will become more refined and a real expression of your artistry.

Assortment of beads available.

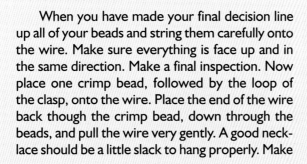

When you have made your final decision line up all of your beads and string them carefully onto the wire. Make sure everything is face up and in the same direction. Make a final inspection. Now place one crimp bead, followed by the loop of the clasp, onto the wire. Place the end of the wire back though the crimp bead, down through the beads, and pull the wire very gently. A good necklace should be a little slack to hang properly. Make one last check for design, placement, and orientation. Now you can put one drop of cement inside the crimp bead. The best cement for this job is Hypo-cement, which has a long insertion needle. Let the cement set for ten minutes. With your crimp pliers carefully compress the crimp beads so that they remain round but fit tightly over the wire.

Assortment of silver clasps.

Construction of necklace.

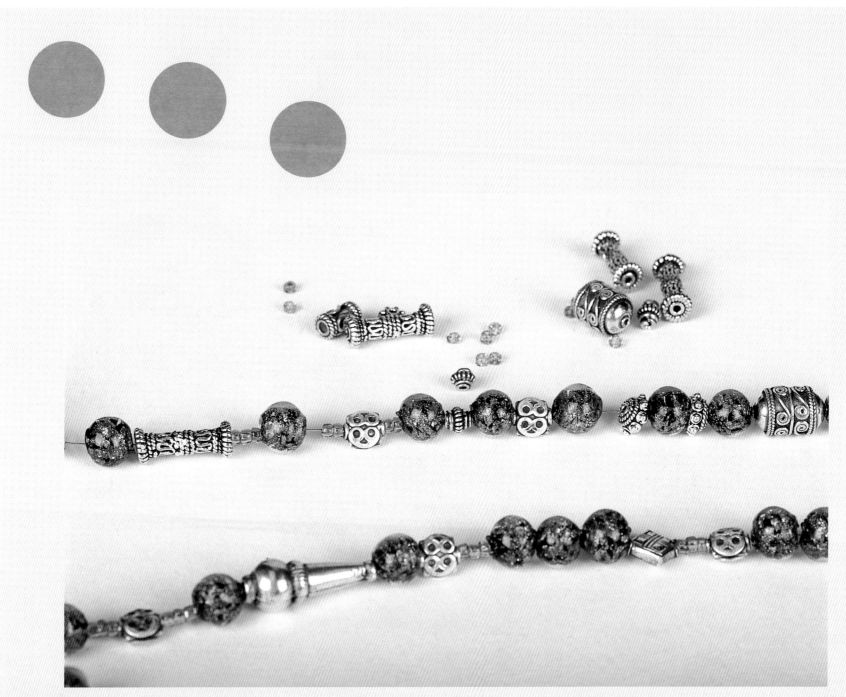

Detail of construction of necklace.

Completed turquoise pendant with other choices.

You are done! Wear your necklace with pride and be prepared for praise and admiration when you say you made it yourself.

Author's necklace titled "Casbah." *Courtesy of Steve Meltzer Photography.*

Detail of author's necklace titled "Kyrenia." *Courtesy of Steve Meltzer Photography.*

Bead Stringing Materials

Tape measure.

Hypo-cement, E-6000, epoxies.

Assorted gems, beads, spacers, crimp beads, clasps, in as many colors, textures, and sizes as possible.

Beadalon or Softflex, a nylon coated wire for stringing beads.

Jeweler's tools. Acquire a basic set of tools slowly, as needed.

Bead crimping pliers.

Hemostat.

Side cutter.

Round nose, flat nose, chain nose pliers.

Needle files.

Tools necessary for bead stringing.

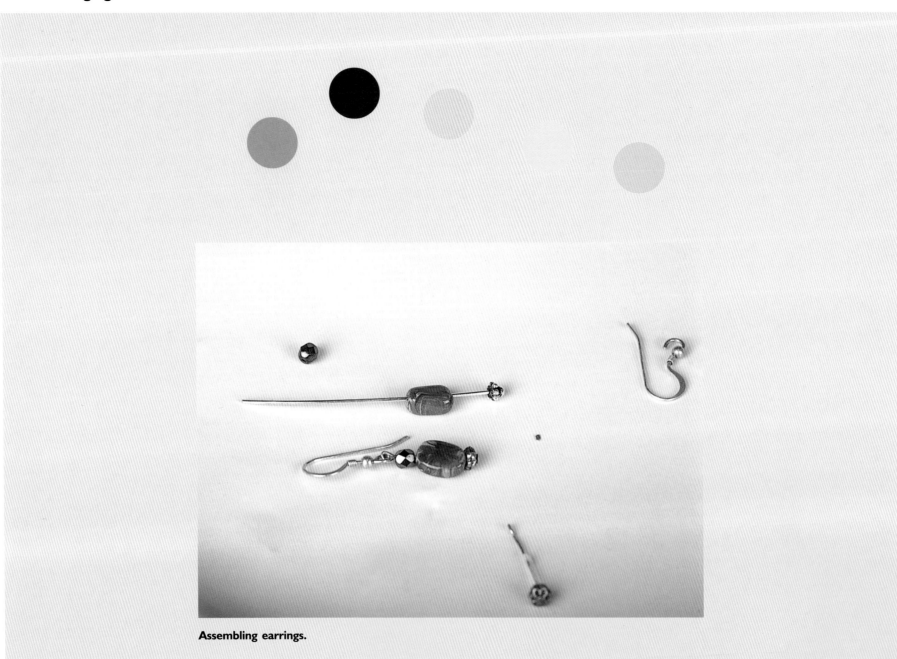

Assembling earrings.

Completed earrings.

Assembling pendants.

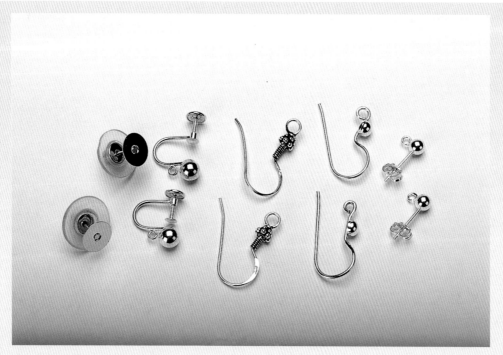

Assortment of earring findings.

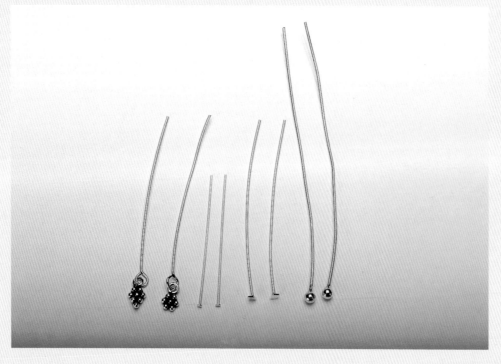

Assortment of head pins.

A Simply Spectacular Bead

We are now going to make a simply spectacular bead. This is a challenging project, and it will be necessary to gather all your knowledge about basic clay working. Please refer to other chapters in this manuscript. The result will be well worth the effort. I suggest that you read this article carefully from beginning to end before starting the project. Be patient and work with me. The beauty of this bead comes from the many different elements that must work together: the design, color selection, and the various components.

You already know about layering techniques. You also know how to make a millefiori bead. Now we will combine those two techniques and add inclusions of clay rolls to an already formed millefiori bead. Remember that clay has very few rules. The cardinal rule is to keep all surfaces moist so that they will adhere. This is extremely important in a complex bead like this, because there are so many elements that have to stick together. Observe closely the examples of finished projects at the end of this chapter. They have been selected carefully so you can see up close just how to create a porcelain inclusion bead necklace.

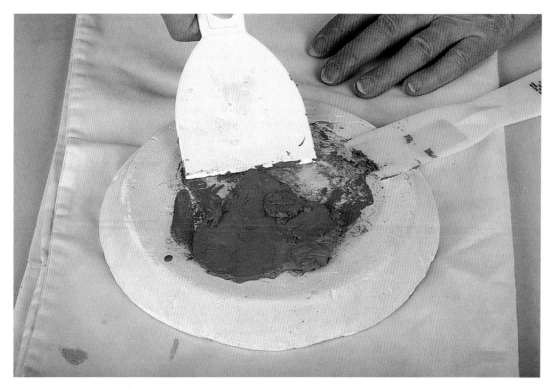

Drying porcelain slurry.

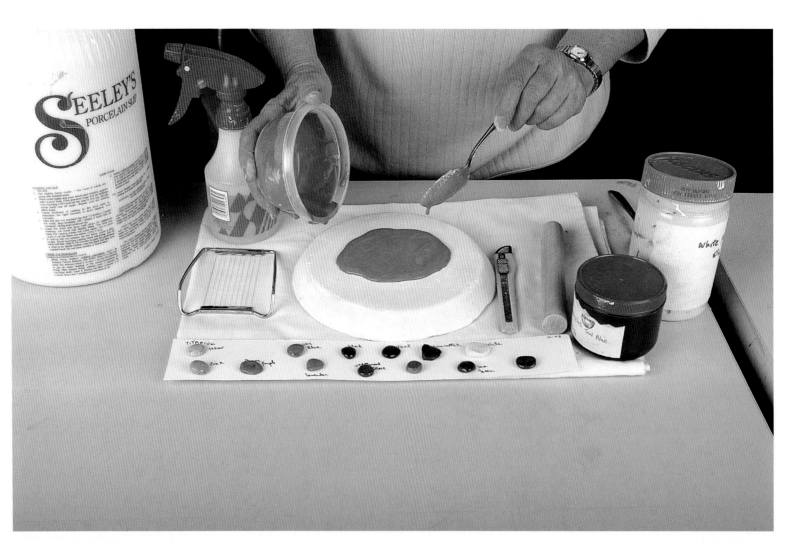

Mixing a color for first layer.

Start with layers of your chosen colors. Build up layers to make a color bar that is 1 inch by 5-inches. Compress the bar so it is firm and every layer is adhered. Trim the edges. Now take those scraps from the trimming and roll them into narrow worms. Slice down into the color bar at 1-1/2, 2-1/2, and 3-1/2-inches. Flatten the worms and insert into the color bar at 1-1/2 inch intervals. Spritz the surfaces so everything will stick together. If you want more contrast, introduce a solid contrasting worm.

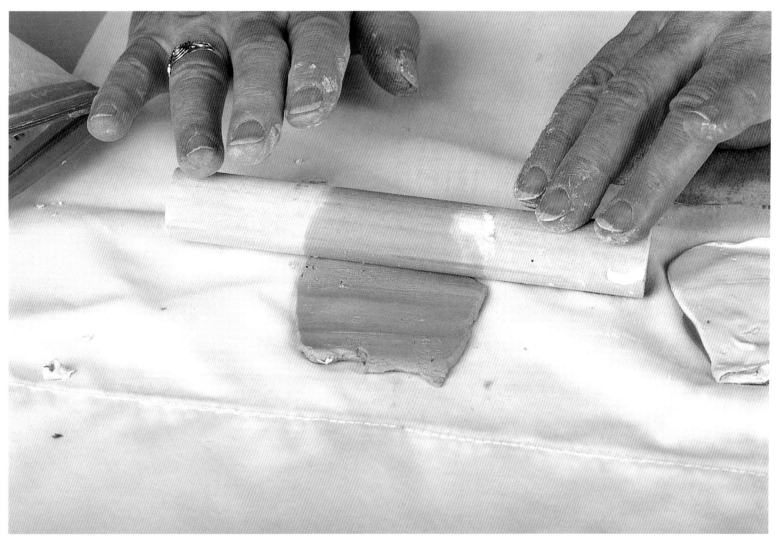

Rolling a layer.

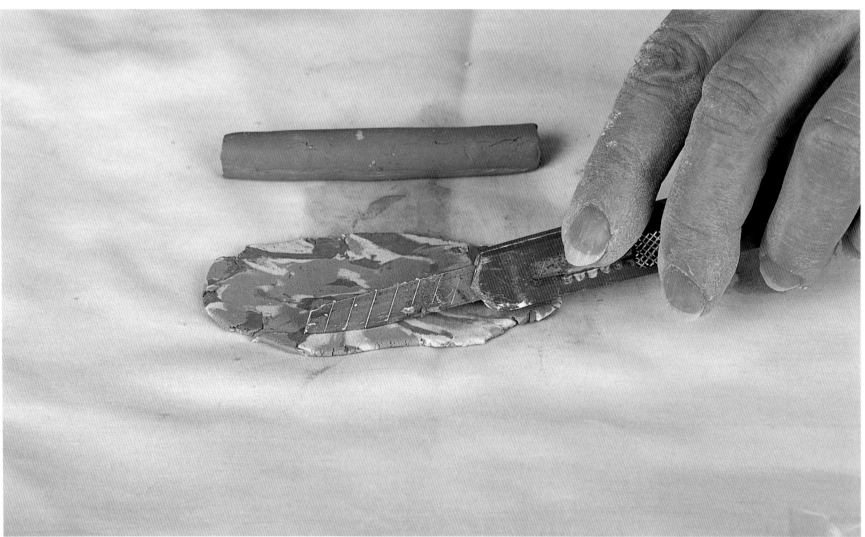

Inserting rolls of porcelain.

Trust me: this will get easier to make with experience! At this point I recommend a frame or wrap. Here's where your ingenuity comes into play. You can introduce new color, pick up an existing color or, for a more unusual look, roll out some of your leftover scrap clay. Each will add interesting design elements to your bead. Roll out a slab that is wide enough and long enough to cover the color bar from end to end. Place the edge of the color bar up against the slab and carefully roll the color bar so that every side is straight and true. All sides will be square. Slice the rough ends off and evaluate your inclusion bar. If you are not pleased with the result, you can slice and add several more narrow worms in different colors to create the image you envisioned. Remember that this is a process and we have to learn the hard way, one step at a time.

Keep your clay covered with plastic sheets, you don't want it to dry out too quickly. Remember to mist. To test for dryness, hold your bead against your cheek. If it feels cool to the touch, it is still too wet. It should be very close to room temperature. Gently roll the piece to maintain the shape and press gently to assure adhesion. Let it firm up a bit. When the roll has a more solid feel to it, carefully slice one end. You will immediately see the color pattern that your bead is developing.

When your beads are ready to fire, set them on clean kiln shelves and fire to Cone 06 (1850 degrees F.). After cooling, they won't be richly colored yet. If you want to see how colorful they will look after they are fired a second time to a much higher heat, dip a bead in water and watch the color emerge. To finish, you can either smooth the rough edges with extra-fine sandpaper, or even better, use a rock tumbler. If you are using a rock tumbler, cover the beads with water, tumble for an hour and test for smoothness. If your beads are still a little rough, tumble for another thirty minutes.

Creating the color bar.

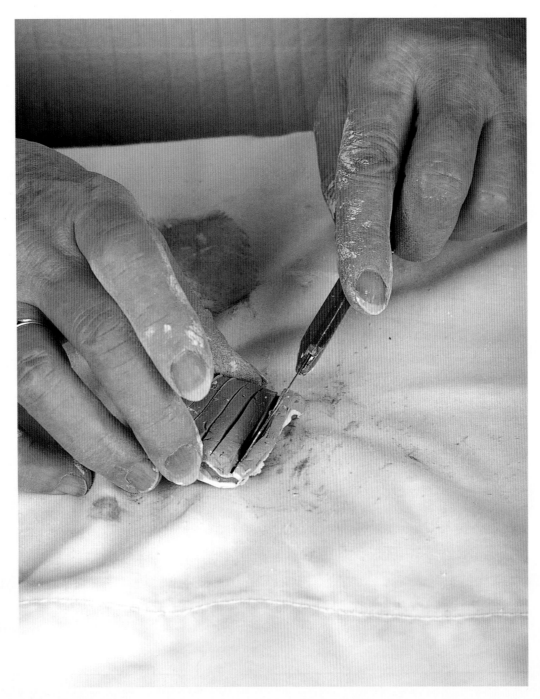

Slicing the color bar.

Preparing the frame around the color bar.

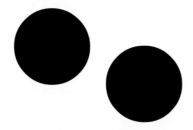

Completing the frame around the color bar.

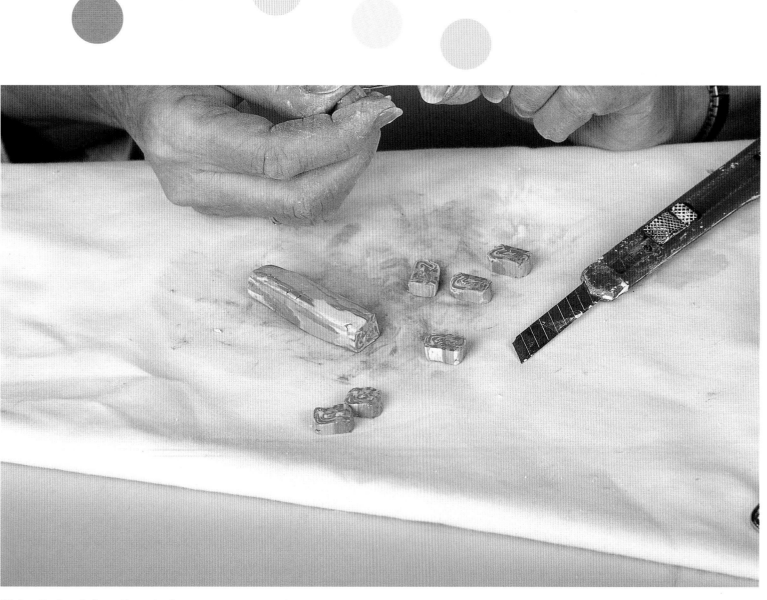

Slicing the beads from the color bar.

Completing the bead process.

Select your best beads. Make sure the holes run completely through. You can't string a bead if it doesn't have a complete hole. Now lay out your best beads, best side up. Brush two layers of clear porcelain glaze on just the top surface. Don't let glaze get into the holes. Make sure there is no glaze on the bottom of the bead. Wipe with a damp sponge if necessary. Fire again to Cone 6 (2250 degrees F.). Let the kiln cool before you open it. The results should produce smiles of delight. You have made a spectacular bead!

Completed necklace, using the beads from the instruction text. "Mixed Message" with five pendants, inclusion, crystal, and Bali beads.

Completed necklace, using another set of inclusion beads. "Summer Storm" with four pendants, inclusion, crystal, and Bali beads.

"Cairo," inclusion necklace with split beads, Bali silver, Swarovski crystals. *Courtesy of Steve Meltzer Photography.*

"Capri," eclectic inclusion beads with variety of layered, millefiori, round beads. Bali and crystal, two pendants. *Courtesy of Steve Meltzer Photography.*

"Sheba," eclectic inclusion beads indicating complexity of design. Bali silver and pink quartz beads. *Courtesy of Steve Meltzer Photography.*

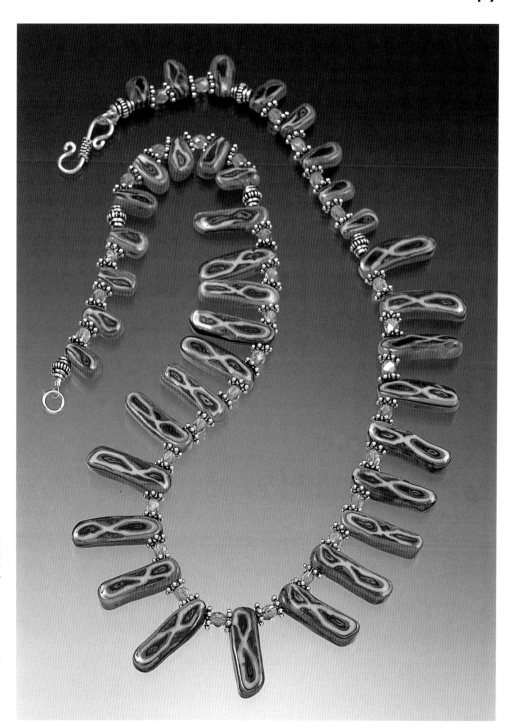

Opposite page:
"Misty Rose," large format inclusion beads with blue carved glass and Bali spacer beads. *Courtesy of Steve Meltzer Photography.*

Right:
"Nefertiti," complex double inclusion bead with Bali spacers and Swarovski crystals. *Courtesy of Steve Meltzer Photography.*

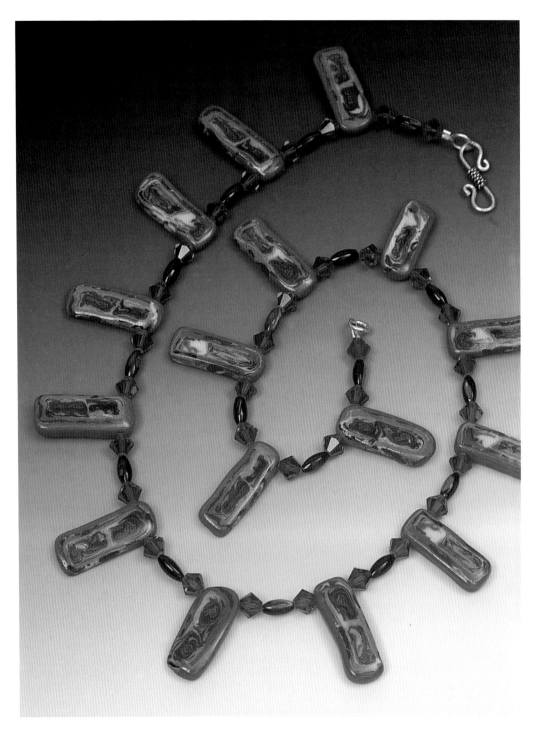

"Helix," double inclusion bead with
silver findings and crystals.

Equipment and Supplies

Small jewelry kiln, equipped with kiln shelves, 1/2" posts, Orton Cones 06, 6. Some choices below.

Aim test kiln, Continental Clay Co., Minneapolis, MN. 1-800-432-CLAY.

Axner test kiln, jewelry kiln or Test plus kiln. Oviedo, FL. 1-800-843-7057.

One gallon container of high fire white porcelain slip. Cone 6 Seeley clay.

High fire glaze, clear. Bailey Ceramics. P.O.B. 1577. Kingston, NY. 1-800-431-6067.

Mason stains in assorted colors. Be certain these can be fired to Cone 6. Check with your supplier. Stable stains from Cerdec/Degussa and most Mason stains are both available from Axner Pottery Supply. Oviedo, FL. 1-800-843-7057.

Plaster work surface. Throwing bats are excellent. I have also used the backside of old molds. Del Val Supply in Wyndmoor, PA has a supply. 215-233-0655.

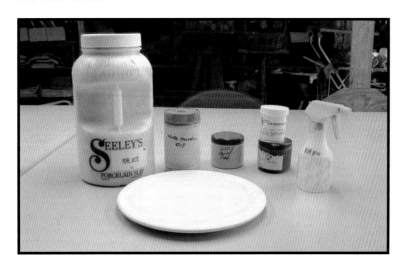

Plastic wrap and sealable bags in pint, quart, and gallon sizes.
Three or four tablespoons.
Wire egg slicer.
Plastic putty scraper.
Small sponges.
6" x 1" dowel or suitable rolling pin.
Long sharp razor blade in retractable holder.
Assorted embroidery and darning needles. Coats and Clarks.
Water mister.
Rock tumbler. Available at Rio Grande Gems. Albuquerque, NM. 1-800-545-6566.
Fine percale or other fine textures for work surface. An old pillowcase is good.
Extra fine sandpaper.

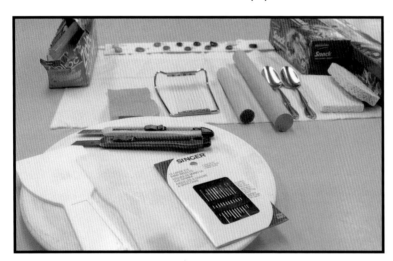

Bead Stringing Materials

Tape measure.
Hypo-cement and other instant glues.
Assorted gems, beads, silver spacers, crimp beads, clasps.
Acculon or Beadalon nylon coated wire in assorted diameters.